Kid's Coding Workbook Series

Code Using Java

First Edition Revision 2

By Troy Tuckett

Java is a product licensed through Oracle Corporation. IntelliJ IDEA is a product licensed through jetbrains.com

ISBN: 9781791550820

Other Books by the Author

Today you can find these additional Kid's Coding Workbooks on Amazon.com

Code Using Scratch (paperback and kindle versions)
Code Using Python (paperback and kindle versions)
Code Using Pseudo Code (paperback and kindle versions)
Create Games Using Scratch (paperback and kindle versions)

Table of Contents

INTRODUCTION

For Parents...

This workbook was written after decades of teaching beginners coding skills. It is meant to teach key principles and cement them in the minds of kids using fun and exciting exercises.

The workbook was created to promote self-paced learning, but it can also be used in a classroom setting. It has two main elements that work together to help kids learn coding. "Learn It!" sections teach a principle in detail and provide examples that are useful to learning the topic. "Try It!" sections then use fun exercises and games to reinforce the learning in the prior section.

For Kids...

It has been my experience that you will learn best when coding concepts are visual and you take time to use your hands to code what you have learned. I strongly encourage you to use this workbook to write out the exercises as explained.

What do you need to know to start?

I am assuming in this book that you have little or no knowledge of coding and no knowledge of Java. I provide every step you need to get started and learn the language.
Because there are some download and install steps, some computer skills and understanding of folders and windows will be helpful. If you don't have them, have a parent help you.

Getting Started with Java

Java is a general-purpose language that is very popular in business. Because of its popularity, it is a great language to learn.

Before you write a program using Java you will need to have the proper software installed. This includes installing an Integrated Development Environment (IDE). A common environment that supports a variety of operating systems is called IntelliJ IDEA. We will be using the Community edition because it installs easy and is free to use.

Here are the steps to get the IDE installed and a short program written.

Begin by going to https://www.jetbrains.com/idea/download/ and selecting "Download" under the Community heading. Once the file is downloaded, click on the install file and follow the install process.

Once the product is installed, find the installed program and double click to run it.

The first time running the program, it might require you answer some questions about where to store files and such. After that, you will end up at the welcome page.

Select "Create New Product" from the welcome page.

Select "Java" from the different types of projects and click

Name your project. I called mine "Stuff" but you can call yours what you like.

With the project created, Select the project folder in the upper left.

From the project tree select the name of your project ("Stuff" for me) and then right click "src" and choose "New" and "Java Class".

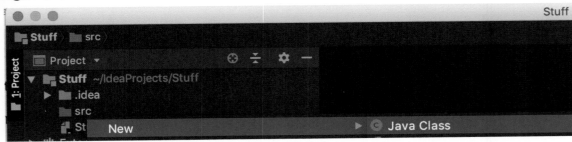

A dialog will pop up where you provide a name for your class. Let's call it "MyClass". Then click OK.

Within the editor on the right side of the page, type the following program, making sure you include all of the elements.

```java
public class MyClass {
    public static void main(String[] args) {
        System.out.println("Hello World");
    }
}
```

When done, right click within the editor and select

▶ Run 'MyClass.main()'   ^⇧R

If everything is set up right, toward the bottom of your IDE you should see the output of.

```
MyClass ×
/Library/Java/JavaVirtualMachines/
Hello World
objc[72596]: Class JavaLaunchHelpe

Process finished with exit code 0
```

If your response looks like this, you are ready to get cracking on coding.

BASIC COMPUTER CONCEPTS

Learn Computer Parts

Learn the most basic parts that make up a computer system.

A computer is made up of three different types of parts:
inputs, processing, and outputs.

No matter what the type of computer—desktop, laptop, smartphone, or other systems—each of these parts are there. Here are some examples of what you might see in these parts of a system.

Input
- Keyboard
- Mouse
- Finger

Processing
- Calculations
- Controls

Output
- Monitor/Screen
- Printer

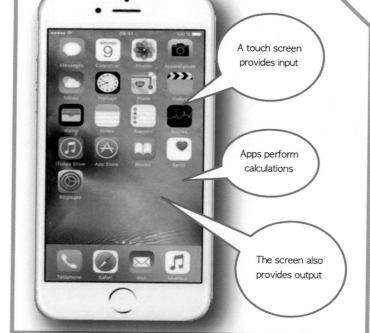

A touch screen provides input

Apps perform calculations

The screen also provides output

These three elements work together to provide the experiences we have come to expect from our computers.

Inputs come into the computer and flow into a processing program where logic and calculations are applied. Once the processing is complete, the results are output. This can happen thousands of times per second.

Examples of Parts

This exercise helps you remember the parts of a computer.

Write down an example of each of these types of parts.

Input

Processing

Output

Learn Input

Learn the different kinds of input that a computer can receive, and what the computer can do with the input.

Inputs are an important part of a computer. They are the way a computer system receives information that is then processed. Once inputs have been processed, outputs can be created.

In the previous lesson we talked about the different kinds of inputs a computer might have. We talked about a small list of inputs, but there are many others.

- Keyboard

- Mouse
- Touch Screen
- File or Database
- Sensors

Input can also be events like a mouse getting clicked or a screen being touched. Inputs can be stored to be used later in your program.

The simple input from the keyboard we will use in examples and exercises is this.

```
variableName = input.next();
```

The **input** statement above stores the keyboard input in a variable called *variableName*. You will learn more about variables later in this workbook.

Try It!

My First Input

This exercise helps you understand the concept of inputs.

Follow these steps to create your first program with inputs.

1. Find the project you created in IntelliJ and right click on **scr**. Select **New** and **Java Class**.

2. Name your class `MyFirstInputProgram` and hit Enter.
3. The file name will appear in the editor area on the right. In that area type

```java
import java.util.Scanner;

public class MyFirstInputProgram {

    public static void main(String[] args) {

        Scanner input = new Scanner(System.in);

        System.out.print("What's your name?");
        input.next();

    }
}
```

4. Now right click in the white area and find **Run 'MyFirstInputProgram.main()'**
5. The output at the bottom of the screen should look like this. You will need to type a name for your program to finish.

```
What's your name? bob
```

Learn It!

Learn Output

Learn the different kinds of output that a computer can send once processing has been completed.

Outputs are the way a computer system shows the results of processing that has happened.

There are a bunch of ways that a computer can provide output. This is a small list, but there are many others.

- Monitor or Screen
- Files or Databases
- Printers
- Other Devices

Without output, we don't know what has happened within the computer program. In the early days of personal computers, the Altair computer would output through a bunch of flashing lights. Today our output seems almost real. We have come a long way since the Altair.

1980

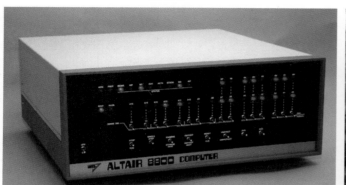

2018

For the examples and exercises in this workbook, we are using a simple screen output like this.

```
System.out.println("This is what is being output.")
```

Most programs today use much better-looking outputs. Windows or Mac programs use a graphical windows output using forms, buttons, fields, and more. The browser on your computer uses a similar output. Video games use a much more complex graphical output. When you print a document to the printer, you are also seeing output from the computer. In fact, the ding of your phone or even when it vibrates are forms of output.

First name:

Mickey

Last name:

Mouse

Submit   Reset

Try It!

My First Output

This exercise helps you understand the concept of outputs.

Follow these steps to create your first program with outputs.

1. Create a new Java Class called "MyFirstOutputProgram" and hit Enter.
2. In the editor area for your new file, type.

```
import java.util.Scanner;

public class MyFirstOutputProgram {

    public static void main(String[] args) {

        Scanner input = new Scanner(System.in);
        String name;

        System.out.println("What's your name?");
        name = input.next();

        System.out.println ("Your name is " + name);

    }
}
```

3. Right click in the editor area and select **Run 'MyFirstOutputProgram'**
4. The output at the bottom of the screen should look like this.

```
What's your name? bob
Your name is bob
```

Learn It!

Learn About Programming Languages

Learn what a programming language does and why we use them.

Computers think in zeros and ones. Humans think in words, sentences and expressions. Programming languages allow us to tell the computer the steps to take using something that is similar to our own language or similar to a game.

There are lots of different programming languages that are good at doing different things. Some of them are more general purpose and others are more specialized.

Once you learn one programming language, it is easier to learn another one.

Coding languages have these 6 basic functions:

1) Take input, 2) Give output, 3) Store variables, 4) Perform calculations, 5) Make branching, and 6) Provide looping.

You have already learned about a couple of these. Throughout this workbook we will learn all of the basic functions of programming languages.

Here are some example statements from different languages.

Language	Statements
| Java | ```
public class HelloWorld {
        public static void main(String[] args){
                System.out.println("Hello World!");
        }
}
``` |
| COBOL | ```
PROCEDURE DIVISION.
DisplayPrompt.
    DISPLAY " Hello World!".
    STOP RUN.
``` |
| C++ | ```
int main()
{
    cout << "Hello World!";
    return 0;
}
``` |
| Basic | ```
10 PRINT "Hello World!"
20 END
``` |
| Python | ```
Print ("Hello World!")
``` |
| Pseudo Code | ```
Display "Hello World!"
``` |
| Scratch | say Hello World! for 2 secs |

Notice how each of these languages does the same thing (print Hello World! to the screen) but in a different way.

In coding we usually call the statements written in a programming language "Source Code" or "Code" for short. We call it this because even though it often looks like English, it is a set of special instructions that tell the computer what to do.

Before source code can be executed by the computer it must first be changed into something the computer understands. Some languages use an interpreter to translate the code on the fly while it is running. This takes the code and puts it into a language the computer can use line by line at run time. A compiler is a little bit different than an interpreter because the code is transformed into a file you can run.

Try It!

Functions of Programming Languages

This exercise helps you learn the basic functions of a programming language.

Fill out the missing pieces about basic functions of programming languages.

Take _ _ _ _ _ _ _ _ _ _ _ _ _ _ _ _ _ _ _   _ _ _ _ _ _ _ _ _ _ _ _ _ _ _ _ _ _ _ **output**

Store _ _ _ _ _ _ _ _ _ _ _ _ _ _ _ _ _ _   _ _ _ _ _ _ _ _ _ _ _ _ _ _ _ _ _ _ **calculations**

Make _ _ _ _ _ _ _ _ _ _ _ _ _ _ _ _ _ _   _ _ _ _ _ _ _ _ _ _ _ _ _ _ _ _ _ **looping**

BASIC CODING PRINCIPLES

Learn Sequencing

Learn the way that a computer interprets and processes a program.

Sequencing means a set of steps one after another.

Here are some of the ideas around how a computer processes a program.

1. One step at a time
2. Top to bottom
3. The only things that break this top to bottom flow are:
   a. Branches
   b. Loops
   c. Objects and Methods

We will discuss these in this workbook. A computer doesn't make guesses like we do. It has to be told in detail every little thing to do.

That level of detail is what a computer needs to know to execute your program.

Simple Exercise

Think about what steps you would have to take to get from one side of a classroom to the other.

1 - Walk three steps ahead

2 - Turn left a half turn

3 - Walk two steps ahead

4 - Turn left a quarter turn

5 - Walk five steps ahead

6 - Stop

Sequencing Example

Here is an example of some steps that show the level of detail you must use to tell the computer what to do.

```
Scanner input = new Scanner(System.in);
String name;I don't
float price1;
float price2;
float price3;
float total;

System.out.print("Please enter your name: ");
name = input.next();
System.out.print("Please enter the price of book 1: ");
price1 = input.nextFloat();
System.out.print("Please enter the price of book 2: ");
price2 = input.nextFloat();
System.out.print("Please enter the price of book 3: ");
price3 = input.nextFloat();
total = price1 + price2 + price3;
System.out.println("Name: " + name + " your total price is: " +
total);
```

I know you aren't going to know what all of this means yet, but from the example you can see the level of detail and number of steps it takes to get stuff done within a program.

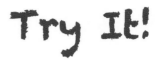

Recipe to Steps

This exercise helps you think through the detailed steps using a recipe.

1. Find a medium sized recipe for food you like to eat. The recipe should have between 5 and 8 steps.
2. Change the recipe into a set of steps written using something like a program.

Step	Instruction
1	
2	
3	
4	
5	
6	
7	
8	

Sequence Exercise

This exercise helps you think through the detailed steps needed to complete a simple task.

Create a set of steps so that the girl moves so that she is standing next to the boy.

Remember: You have to tell the computer exactly what to do.

Step	Instruction
1	
2	
3	
4	
5	
6	
7	
8	

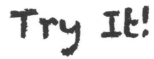

My First Sequence

This exercise helps you think through the detailed steps needed to complete a simple task.

You've already written a program with a very short sequence of two steps. Follow the below steps to create your first sequence program with more steps.

1. Create a new Java class called "MyFirstSequenceProgram" and hit Enter.
2. In the editor area for your new file, type.

```java
import java.util.Scanner;
public class MyFirstSequenceProgram {
  public static void main(String[] args) {
    Scanner input = new Scanner(System.in);
    String name;
    String address;
    String phone;
    int age;

    System.out.print("What's your name? ");
    name = input.nextLine();
    System.out.print("What's your address? ");
    address = input.nextLine();
    System.out.print("What's your phone number? ");
    phone = input.nextLine();
    System.out.print("What's your age? ");
    age = input.nextInt();

    System.out.println("Your name is " + name + " your address
      is " + address + " your phone number is " + phone + " your
      age is " + age);
  }
}
```

3. Right click in the editor area and select **Run 'MyFirstSequenceProgram'**
4. The output at the bottom of the screen should look like this.

```
What's your name? bob
What's your address? 123 Main Street
What's your phone number? 5551234
What's your age? 15
Your name is bob your address is 123 Main Street your phone
number is 5551234 your age is 15
```

Learn the Coding Process

Learn how to do coding using a simple and standard process.

We have learned so far that coding is about putting a bunch of lines of code together in a sequence to complete some kind of a task.

To be able to know what statements need to go together, you first need to understand what problem you are solving. You get this from something called requirements.

An example of requirements might be something like this.
Show the sum of 4 numbers that you get as input from the user.

Now you need to decide how you are going to meet the requirements. To do this, you will write out a set of high-level steps.

An example of these steps would be something like this:

1. Ask the user for first number and store in variable1
2. Ask the user for second number and store in variable2
3. Ask the user for third number and store in variable3
4. Ask the user for fourth number and store in variable4
5. Add up the numbers and store in total
6. Display the total

After you have the steps down and have walked through them a couple of times to make sure they are correctly arranged, it is time to change these steps into a program.

The Java code for the above steps would look something like.

```
Scanner input = new Scanner(System.in);
int variable1;
```

```
int variable2;
int variable3;
int variable4;
int total;

System.out.print("What is the first number you want to add? ");
variable1 = input.nextInt();
System.out.print("What is the second number you want to add? ");
variable2 = input.nextInt();
System.out.print("What is the third number you want to add? ");
variable3 = input.nextInt();
System.out.print("What is the forth number you want to add? ");
variable4 = input.nextInt();

total = variable1 + variable2 + variable3 + variable4;
System.out.println("The total of the four numbers is " + total);
```

Notice the linkage between the requirements, steps, and the Java code. The code has much more specific details.

Learn It!

Learn Variables

Learn how temporary data is stored in computer memory and then brought back when needed.

Sometimes we need to store some numbers or other data to be used later as we write our program. This temporary data is stored in things called "Variables".

Have you ever been to the post office? Inside the post office is a wall of mailboxes. Think of a variable as one of these mailboxes. At your post office visit, you might have noticed that the mailboxes come in different shapes and sizes.

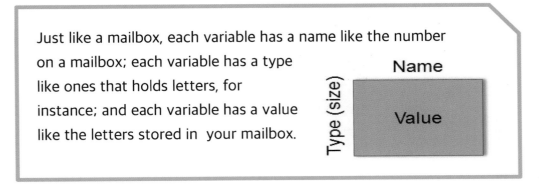

Just like a mailbox, each variable has a name like the number on a mailbox; each variable has a type like ones that holds letters, for instance; and each variable has a value like the letters stored in your mailbox.

When it comes to using variables, here are a few rules that you will need to learn and follow.

- Declare variables before you use them
- When you declare a variable, specify its name and type
- You can change the value of a variable throughout your program (thus the name "variable")
- The type of the variable affects more than just the size. Different types of variables store different categories of data within them. Some common types are.
  - int - A number without a decimal point
  - float - A number with a decimal point
  - String - Multiple characters and numbers together
  - char - A single letter or other character
  - Boolean - True or False

Here is what it looks like to declare a variable.

```
Type        Name
int   myVariable
```

Here is what it looks like to store data within a variable.

```
Name        Initialize
myVariable   = 10
```

Here is what it looks like to retreive data from a variable.

```
System.out.println("The number is: " + myVariable)
```

This line shows a string of "The number is: " and gets the value from *myVariable,* converts it to a **String** type and adds it to the output.

Try It!

Matching types

This exercise helps you to learn different types of variables.

Draw a line to match the value with the correct variable type.

A - Single letter

100 - Number between 0 and 100

2.50 - Number with a decimal

Cat - A word or sentence

TRUE - A true or a false

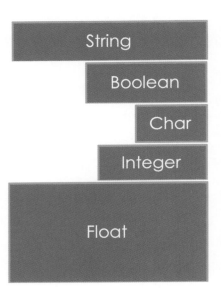

Try It!

My First Variable

This exercise helps you learn about using variables in your programs.

Follow these steps to create your first program that uses a variable.

1. Create a new Java Class called "MyFirstVariableProgram" and hit Enter.
2. In the editor area for your new file, type.

```
public class MyFirstVariableProgram {
```

```
public static void main(String[] args) {
    int myNumber;
    myNumber = 10;

    System.out.print("Your number is " + myNumber);
}
}
```

3. Right click in the editor area and select **Run 'MyFirstVariableProgram'**
4. The output at the bottom of the screen should look like this.
   ```
   Your number is 10
   ```

My First Program

This exercise tests your skills at writing your first program using variables and the coding process.

In previous exercises, I have given you the steps to creating a program. This will be your first program you do completely on your own.

Refer to the earlier examples and the Java Reference at the end of the workbook to help you write your first Java program.

Here are the requirements. *Show a word that was input by the user.*

Steps
First, write down the high-level steps you will take to meet the requirements.

_____

1 _____

2 _____

3 _____

_____

4 _____

5 _____

Go into the Java IDE and create this program.

Learn Arithmetic Expressions

Learn how to use variables and operations together to create arithmetic expressions.

It is very common when writing a program that you will need to do something more involved than just store values in variables. Here we will learn the principles around arithmetic expressions that are found in programs.

When we set or change a variable, we can also add arithmetic expressions to the line. Here is an example of setting a value and an arithmetic expression.

```
total = (number1 + number2) + (number3 * number4)
```

In coding, multiplication is usually done using a * and division is usually done using a /.

The sky's the limit on the different types of arithmetic expressions you can perform. In addition to simple + - x and ÷, most languages also include functions to handle more complex operations including exponents, square root, trigonometry operations, and some business operations.

Here are a couple of common mathmatical operations written as arithmetic expressions in a program.

```
a = cmath.sqrt(math.pow(r,2)
K = b * (cmath.sqrt(4* math.pow(a,2) - math.pow(b,2)) / 4
mean = sumOfTheTerms / numberOfDiffTerms
speed = totalDistance / totalTime
pythagorean = math.pow(a,2) + math.pow(b,2) - math.pow(c,2)
```

When writing your arithmetic expressions, you need to consider the mathematical order of operations. Below are some of these rules:

Rule 1:	First perform any calculations inside parentheses.
Rule 2:	Next perform all multiplication and division, working from left to right.
Rule 3:	Lastly, perform all addition and subtraction, working from left to right.

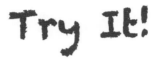

Create A Calculator

This exercise helps you learn about variables and arithmetic expressions using a calculator program.

Write a program that creates a simple calculator that adds and subtracts two numbers using the below details

1. Ask the user to provide two numbers
2. Perform the calculation (either add or subtract)
3. Display the result

Go into the Java IDE and create this program.

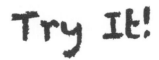

Change Fahrenheit to Celsius

This exercise helps you learn about variables and arithmetic expressions using a program that calculates Celsius.

Write a program that changes a temperature from Fahrenheit to Celsius using the following details.

1. Ask the user for a number in Fahrenheit
2. Change the number to Celsius using the below formula.
3. Display the answer in Celsius

Formula:
```
celsius = (fahrenheit - 32) x 5/9
```

Extra Credit: Write another program that changes from Celsius to Fahrenheit using this formula.

Formula:
```
fahrenheit = celsius x (9/5) + 32
```

Go into the Java IDE and create this program.

House Payment Calculator

This exercise helps you learn about variables and arithmetic expressions using a program that calculates a monthly house payment.

Given:
```
Loan Principle = 200000
Annual Interest Rate = 6.5% (use .065)
Term of Loan= 30 years
```

Monthly payment calculation:
```
payment=(principle/((1/interest rate)-(1/(interest rate * Math.pow(1
+ interest rate, -months)))))
```

Pow is a Java function that calculates exponent.

Write a program that calculates monthly payment and displays it as output.

Go into the Java IDE and create this program.

MORE CODING PRINCIPLES

- -

Learn It!

Learn Branching

Learn the most basic concepts around branching within a computer program.

Computers are really good at making decisions, but we have to tell the computer the rules around how to make these decisions.

Branches, also called conditional statements, allow a program to take more than one route. The computer uses a logical expression to decide which route to take.

A logical expression resolves to True or False. Here are some of the elements of logical expressions:

Equality	"abc" == "abc"
Inequality	"abc" != "def"
AND	(100 AND 200) > 50
OR	(100 OR 200) > 50
NOT	NOT (100 > 50)

If you wanted to write a logical expression that decides if you can go to a PG-13 movie, it might look like this.

```
(myAge > 12)
```

To be able to go to a PG-13 movie, you need to be older than 12.

This logical expression would return false for some of you but might return true for some of us who are older than 12.

Conditions

In its most simple form, branching has one route but two outcomes. When the logical expression is true the program goes down one path and when it is false, it skips over the true path. A simple condition with these routes looks like this.

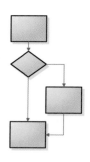

```
if (logical expression){
     Do something if true
}
```

A more complex form of a branching has more than one route. It looks like this.

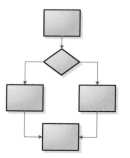

```
if (logical expression) {
   Do something if true
} else {
 Do something if false
}
```

In the above case the true condition goes down the first route, and the false condition goes down the second route (after the **else**).

There are times when you even need a more complex version of branching. You might have three or more routes to take. In Java branching with three routes looks like this.

```
if (logical expression){
   Do something if true
} if (another logical expression){
   Do something if the first expression is false and this
   one is true.
} else {
```

```
  Do something if both are false
}
```

You can also put the **if** and **if-else** inside of other blocks of code as needed.

Here is an example of a simple program that uses branching. We will use the PG-13 example we talked about earlier in this section.

```java
import java.util.*;
public class BranchClass {
  public static void main(String[] args) {
    Scanner input = new Scanner(System.in);
    System.out.print("How old are you? ");
    int age = input.nextInt();
    if (age > 13 || age == 13) {
      System.out.println("You are old enough to attend a PG-13
      movie.  Please talk to your parents.");
    } else {
      System.out.println("Sorry that you aren't old enough to
      go to a PG-13 movie.");
    }
  }
}
```

In the above example we ask the user for their age and store it in a variable called *age*. We then use an **if-else** statement where we test if the users age is greater than 13 or equal to 13. If this test is true, we display a message that the person is old enough to attend. Otherwise we display a message that the person cannot attend.

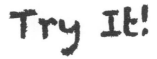

Find Positive Numbers

This exercise helps you learn about arithmetic expressions and branching using a program that finds positive numbers.

Write a program that decides whether a number provided by the user is positive or negative using the below details.

1. Ask user for a number
2. Decide if the number is positive or negative

3. Display one message if it is positive and another if it is negative.

Go into the Java IDE and create this program.

Try It!

Guessing Game Round One

This exercise helps you learn branching and logical expressions by creating a simple guessing game.

Write a guessing game program using the below details.

- Start with a mystery number
- Ask someone else to guess it
- Tell them if their guess was too high or too low
- Display the results

Go into the Java IDE and create this program.

Learn It!

Learn Looping

Learn the basic concepts around looping statements in a program.

In addition to branching, computers are also great at doing the same thing over and over again. In coding this is often referred to as looping.

Looping statements allow a portion of your program to execute more than once. In a way, it is like a dog chasing its tail.

©Warren Photographic

Here are a couple of the most often used looping statements:

```
for (int count = 0; count<10; count++)
while (count < 10)
```

The **while** loop uses logical expressions like you used with branching.

When it comes to loops, there are usually two basic types. Use this information to decide when and how to use them.

For loop	While loop
Used when you know how many times you will iterate through the loop before the loop starts.	Use when you need to use a logical expression to decide when the loop will end. In most cases you don't know how many iterations it will go through.
The **for** loop has a variable and a set of elements associated with it. In this below example we see a variable called counter is declared and initialized to 0. It will increase by 1 until it is no longer less than 10.	The **while** loop has an external control that can be a counter or can be another type of control used in a logical expression. The logical expression, using the control, must become false during the loop.
`for (int count=0; count<10; count++)`	`isDone = false;` `while (!isDone)`

Here is a quick example of using a **while** loop. We would like to add up 10 numbers the user specifies. Here is what it would look like.

```
import java.util.*;
public class LoopClass {
  public static void main(String[] args) {
     Scanner input = new Scanner(System.in);
     int count = 0;
     int total = 0;

     while (count < 10) {

         System.out.println("Enter a number to add: ");
         int number = input.nextInt();
         total = total + number;
         count ++;
     }
     System.out.println("The total of the numbers is " + total);
  }
}
```

In this program we go through the loop 10 times (0 through 9). Each time we loop, we ask the user for a number, we grab the number typed and put it in a variable called *number* and we add the number to our accumulated *total*. The *count* variable keeps track of how many times we have been through the loop, so we also have to add one to it each time through. Once we are done, we display the *total*.

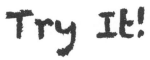

Guessing Game Round Two

This exercise helps you learn more about branching and looping by expanding our guessing game.

Enhance the guessing game by adding the following new requirements to your existing program.

- In the previous program the user got one guess. We want them to guess until they reach the correct answer
- What will you use to end the loop?

- What kind of a loop will you use?

By the way, you can use this function to calculate a random number for your mystery number. **random.nextInt(10)** calculates random number between 0 and 10

Go into the Java IDE and create this program.

Try It!

Rock, Paper, Scissors

This exercise helps you learn more about branching and looping through the Rock Paper Scissors game.

Write a program that uses the Rock, Paper, Scissors rules below.

Run a set number of matches but keep trying after that number while the players are tied.

RPS Rules
Rock crushes Scissors
Scissors cut Paper
Paper covers Rock
No one wins if the two are the same

Go into the Java IDE and create this program.

Russian Roulette

This exercise helps you learn branching and looping as you create Russian Roulette.

Russian Roulette is where a person takes a revolver with a single bullet in it. They spin the cylinder, aim the gun at a target, and pull the trigger.

Create a program that creates the Russian Roulette practice using the below details.

1. The location of the bullet in the six chamber revolver is selected at random
2. The cylinder is spun and the selected chamber is decided at random
3. The gun is aimed at the target and the trigger is pulled
4. The result is displayed to the user
5. The user is asked if they want to try again
6. If so, the trigger is pulled again

Go into the Java IDE and create this program.

Testing the Coding Process

Consider how testing fits within our simple and standard process.

Earlier in this workbook we talked about the coding process. Using this process helps you to think step by step as you try to solve a problem. When we talked about the process earlier, we hadn't talked about branching and looping. Both of these can make it hard to think through the right steps.

In addition to the three steps listed below, I would also suggest that you then test your program's logic (does the program match the requirements).

Remember the coding process we went through earlier:
- Think about the requirements of your program.
- Write down the high-level steps needed to meet the requirements.
- Create your program following these steps.

Here is a simple way you can test your logic.

1) Get yourself a blank piece of paper.
2) Write the variable names in your program across the top of the paper. If you are using looping, there aren't always variable names, but you should include each of them across the top as well. Call them Loop1, Loop2, etc. If you have arrays (we cover them next in the workbook), you should also include these.
3) Now, run through your program step by step. Don't run the program, but walk through the steps as you look at the program.
4) Write down the value of each variable on the paper. Write down the value of each of the loops. When the value changes, write the new value below the previous one.
5) Toward the bottom of the paper write down the output of your program.

Doing this will help you make sure the logic of the steps are correct. It will help you to make sure you have correctly thought through the process.

Here is an example of how to do this. We will use this program from our Sequencing topic.

```java
import java.util.*;
public class ProcessTest {
   public static void main(String[] args) {
      Scanner input = new Scanner(System.in);
      String name;
      float price1;
      float price2;
      float price3;
      float total;

      System.out.print("What's you name? ");
      name = input.next();
      System.out.print("Please enter the price of book 1 ");
      price1 = input.nextFloat();
      System.out.print("Please enter the price of book 2 ");
      price2 = input.nextFloat();
```

```
System.out.print("Please enter the price of book 3 ");
price3 = input.nextFloat();
total = price1 + price2 + price3;
System.out.println("Your name is " + name + " and your total is
" + total);
    }
}
```

Variables

Name	Price1	Price2	Price3	Total
Bob				
	123			
		234		
			345	
				702

Outputs

Your name is Bob and your total is 702

Notice how the value of each variable is updated on the piece of paper as each line is stepped through. Also notice how the output is included at the bottom of the paper.

As you take the time to test in this way, you will better understand what your program is doing and whether it has the right steps to solve the problem.

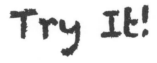

Fibonacci Numbers

This exercise helps you use the coding process with the Fibonacci sequence.

A scientist named Fibonacci was trying to calculate how many rabbits he could raise over time. Create a program that calculates the Fibonacci sequence using these details.

1. Ask user for how many numbers they would like to display
2. Calculate each element of the Fibonacci sequence using the below information:

a. The sequence is 1, 1, 2, 3, 5, 8, 13, 21. . . .

b. The sequence always starts with 1. Then you take 1 and add it to 1 and you get 2. 1 + 2 equals 3, 2 + 3 equals 5, 3 + 5 equals 8, etc.

3. Display each element until the desired number of elements has been reached.

Remember to use the coding process we have just covered. Once you have created your program, use the testing process we just talked about to make sure your program correctly calculates the Fibonacci sequence.

Go into the Java IDE and create this program.

Find a School

This exercise helps you use the coding process by writing a program that finds the correct type of school.

Write a program that decides which type of school a student should attend based on their age using the below details.

1. Ask user for their age
2. Use this table to decide which school the user should attend.

Ages	School
5 - 11	Elementary
12 - 14	Jr. High
15 - 18	High School
> 18	Graduated

3. Display the output as follows:

"Because you are X years old, you go to Y."

Like in the previous exercise, remember to use the coding process we have just covered. Once you have created your program, use the testing process we just talked about to make sure your program correctly finds the right school.

Go into the Java IDE and create this program.

Learn It!

Learn Arrays

Learn what arrays are and how you would use them in your program.

Arrays are used when you need many of the same type of variable. They are often used when you don't know how many variables you need until your program is running.

An array is a set of variables of the same type. Like variables (since an array is a special kind of variable), each array has…a name, a type (size), a set of values (what is in it), and each element has an index to be used to reference it.

Before you can use an array, you must first declare it like this.

```
int myArray[] = {1,2,3,4,5};
```

This example creates an array of 5 integers that are specified when you declare it.

If you don't know the values when writing the code because you are going to calculate them or ask the user to input them, you can declare your array like this.

```
int myArray2[] = new int[10];
```

This example creates an empty array. You now need to fill it with values. A **for** loop is often used in connection with an array. See how we would fill an array with values using a loop.

> The table below shows an array of names with 5 elements.
>
> | Index | Value |
> |-------|-------|
> | 0 | Bob |
> | 1 | Anna |
> | 2 | Jim |
> | 3 | Sandy |
> | 4 | Debbie |

```
for (int count=0; count<10; count++) {
  myArray2[count]=count*100;
}
```

The above example loops 10 times (0 to 9) and adds an array element with a value calculated using (*count* * 100). Notice that it uses count as an index to specify the element to set.

Here is another example that uses two indexes to store a set of people's names and phone numbers.

```
import java.util.*;
public class ArrayExample {
  public static void main(String[] args) {
     Scanner input = new Scanner(System.in);
     String nameArray[] = new String[10];
     String phoneArray[] = new String[10];

     for (int index=0; index<10; index++) {

        System.out.print("Please enter a name ");
        nameArray[index] = input.nextLine();

        System.out.print("Please enter a phone number ");
        phoneArray[index[ = input.nextLine();

     }

     for (int index=0; index<10; index++) {
        System.out.println("Name: " + nameArray[index]
```

```
                  + " Phone: " + phoneArray[index])

        }
    }
}
```

In the above example we collect both *name* and *phone* within the first loop and store them in their respective arrays using the *index* variable to reference their index. Then, we loop again to **println** the value for *name* and *phone* for each array element. Using two arrays in this way is called parallel arrays.

Calculate Average Number

This exercise helps you learn more about branching, looping, and arrays as you create a program that calculates the average of several numbers.

Write a program that calculates the average of a set of numbers using the following details:

1. Ask the user for each of 10 numbers
2. Store each of the numbers in an array
3. Once you have the 10 numbers stored, loop through the array and calculate the average for the numbers
4. Display the results

Average is calculated using this formula.

```
        average = sumOfNumbers / numberOfItems
```

Go into the Java IDE and create this program.

Magic 8-Ball

This exercise helps you learn more about branching, looping, and arrays by creating the Magic 8-Ball as a program.

Write a program that creates the Magic 8-Ball

- Shake the ball and ask a question
- The ball chooses an answer for you
- Answers are chosen randomly
- The ball stores 10 different answers. Use an array to store the answers

Note: You can use this function to calculate a random number. random.nextInt(10) calculates random number between 1 and 10

Answers
Ask again later
Cannot predict now
Very Hazy. Try again
Don't count on it
Most likely
Outlook is good
My sources say no
Better not tell you now
Definitely yes
Outlook is not so good

Go into the Java IDE and create this program.

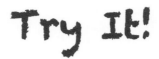

My Media Collection

This exercise helps you learn arrays using a media collection.

Many of you love music. Like you, I have a lot of different music. Because I'm old, this music is stored on media like cassettes, records, and CDs.

You are tasked with creating a collection of media. You will want to use an array to store the media.

Put together a program that creates the media collection as described above. It will need to give me a way to add more media to my collection and view the items I already have.

Go into the Java IDE and create this program.

ADVANCED CODING PRINCIPLES

- -

Learn Methods

Learn the concept of methods, provide examples of the two types of methods, and introduce recursion.

Modular coding is all about breaking a program into logical pieces that are grouped together to form a method. The method can take input parameters and will either do something or return something. Because it is bundled in its own package, it can be developed and tested on its own and reused as needed.

Before you can use a method, it needs to be defined. The first line of the definition tells the computer more about the method. Like declaring a variable, the first line tells the computer the access of the method, the type of the method, the name of the method, and if there are any parameters. Until we get to Objects, we will treat the methods as "static". That just means that we are going to uses them within the class rather than in an object. You will learn more about that later. All you need to know at this point is to include the word "static" after the accessor.

Accessor (public, protected, private)	Static (static or blank)	Type (void means no value returned, or a real type)	Name	Parameters (A comma delimited list with type and name)
public	static	void	myMethod	(parameterName)

Next, you need to write the steps that the method will perform. You can use all of the different coding elements we have discussed so far in this workbook.

Here is a simple example of a method.

```
public static void printNumbers() {
    for (int count=1; count=10; count++)
        System.out.println(count);
}
```

This simple method runs through a loop from 1 to 10 and displays the numbers. Here is a simple example of a method that returns a value.

```
public static int returnNumber(int startValue) {
    int total = startValue
    for (int count=1; count=10; count++) {
        total = total + count;

    return total;
}
```

Like the earlier example, the one above also runs through a loop from 1 to 10. It takes in a parameter (we will talk about those in a minute) and calculates a total which is then returned back to the calling line of your program using the **return** statement.

Parameters

Using parameters is a way to send a value to a method while you are using it. This value is then used just like a populated variable within the method. In the last example above, a value is passed into the *returnNumber()* method. Within the method the value can be used through the *startValue* variable. Notice how in the first line we set *total* to the value of *startValue*.

Using a Method

Defining methods is great, but you then need to use them in your program. This is done by "calling" the method. To call a method that returns a value, you will treat it exactly like a variable in an arithmetic expression like this.

```
myNumber = MyClass.returnNumber(123);
```

Remember we named our method *returnNumber()* and we pass a value in the parameter array of 123. This is then used within the method itself.

When the method doesn't return a value, you call it without including it in an arithmetic expression like this.

```
MyClass.printNumbers();
```

Recursion

In addition to using a method from your program, you can also call methods from within that method. When you call the method you are in, this is called recursion.

In a simple example, we will display a set of messages similar to using a loop but will use recursion instead.

```
public static void showMessage(int numberOfTimes) {
    if (numberOfTimes > 0) {
        System.out.println("Printing a recurring message ");
        showMessage(numberOfTimes -1);
    }
}
```

The **if** statement is really important because without it the program would loop forever.

See the line in the method that calls *showMessage()*? That is what makes this a recursion. If you were to call this method from your program as follows,

```
MyClass.showMessage(5);
```

the method would call itself 5 times and display the message "Printing a recurring message" five times before ending.

There are many reasons to use a recursion. We will explore more within the exercises.

Factorial

This exercise will help you learn recursion and methods using the factorial formula.

The factorial formula is a great way to learn recursion. 5 factorial, also written as 5! is calculated as follows.

```
factorial = 1 * 2 * 3 * 4 * 5
```

Write a factorial method that takes an integer as a parameter. It will need to return a value. The method will then execute recursively until it has looped through the number of times spelled out in the parameter. When it is done, the method should return results.

Note: Make sure you include an **If** statement that allows the recursion to break out or it will run forever.

Go into the Java IDE and create this program.

Try It!

Guessing Game using Methods
This exercise will help you learn methods as you refactor the guessing game.

We have used the Guessing Game idea in a couple of previous exercises. For this exercise, refactor (improve on) the Guessing Game by breaking some of the code into separate methods. Try to use at least two methods you created when updating the game.

Go into the Java IDE and create this program.

Learn It!

Learn Objects
Learn what objects are and how to do coding using them.

Working with objects can be an incredible way of coding. Object-oriented coding involves three basic tenets:

- Encapsulation
- Inheritance
- Polymorphism

We will get into these tenets in sections that follow. For now, let's talk about objects in general.

There are two things you need to visualize about objects. The first is a class and the other is an object.

CLASS	OBJECT
Defines the "blueprint" of a type of object.	Implements the blueprint into a usable object.

We write the general functionality of our program within classes and then create an instance of that class (called an object) that we then use.

Here is what the code looks like to create a class:

```
public class Car {
    String color = "";

    public void displayInformation() {
        System.out.println("The color of this car is " +
        color);
    }
}
```

In the code above we define our class. This is like creating a new type called *Car*. In this class, we define a variable called *color* and we define a method called *displayInformation()*. Notice that this method is a little different from the ones we looked at in the previous section. In this example and the rest of them in this workbook, there will not be a "static" indicator. Below we will create an object that we will refer to rather than the class name.

In Java the .Java file and the class name need to match exactly, including the case (upper and lower case). I suggest that you right click on **src** and create a new Java Class for each of these examples. Be careful to make sure the file matches the class name.

If you wanted to use this class, you will need to create an object instance of the class like this.

```
Car myCar = new Car();
```

With the object instance created, you can now use the object as follows.

```
myCar.color = "Red";
myCar.displayInformation();
```

The last statement above would produce output like this.

```
The color of this car is Red
```

The one last thing we need to talk about is a special kind of method called a **constructor**. The constructor is a way to set up the values of an object at the time it is created. The only thing really different here is what we name the method. A constructor has the same name as the class. Let's take our *Car* class and add the constructor:

```
public class Car {
    String color= "";

    //This is the constructor
    public Car(String tempColor) {
        color = tempColor;
    }

    public void displayInformation() {
        System.out.println("The color of this car is "
            + color);
    }
}
```

Once the constructor is defined, we can then use it like this.

```
Car myCar = new Car("Yellow");
```

See how we set the *color* to Yellow at the time we create the object instance?

These are the very basics of objects. In the next several lessons we will delve into the topic in more detail.

Try Objects

This exercise helps you learn object coding using a simple program.

Using the previous lesson and the examples contained therein create a program with these requirements,

- Create a class using something of your choosing. Define at least one variable and one method within the class
- Write the code that would be used to create an object instance of the class you created above
- Write a snippet of code that would use the object you created above

Go into the Java IDE and create this program.

Learn Encapsulation

Learn about encapsulation, one of the tenets of object-oriented coding.

Encapsulation is about bundling data and operations into a single package. Doing this allows us to better manage our program in a couple of ways.

First, it allows you to manage the scope of change when it comes to variables within the class and the operations (methods) that affect that data.

We haven't really used an accessor yet, but they determine the visibility of a class, variable, or method. The **public** accessor allows the element to be visible to all other classes inside and outside the class. **Protected** allows only classes within the inheritance hierarchy to see the element. **Private** restricts visibility to the element only within the class. When we set a variable as **private**, we can ensure any changes to variable data must come through methods in the class.

```java
public class Car {
    private String color = "";

    public Car(String tempColor) {
        color = tempColor;
    }

    public void displayInformation() {
        System.out.println("Car: The color of this car is "
                + color);
    }
}
```

Second, when it comes to testing the class, you can do it as a single unit, which is the basis for unit testing. Keeping the changes and the tests focused on a single class allow you to manage the impacts that change has on the data and operations.

It is considered a best practice to use encapsulation as shown in the **Car** example above to ensure access and scope are closely managed.

Learn It!

Learn Inheritance

Learn about inheritance, one of the tenets of object-oriented coding.

Inheritance is something we see all around us. In your own family you inherit certain traits from your father and mother. If you have a sibling, that person likewise inherits traits. Classes can have inheritance in a similar way to that of your family.

In coding we call the parent the "super" class. Other classes can inherit from the super class. Those that inherit from the super are called "sub" classes.

Let's look at some examples. Let's use the *Car* class we've seen in previous lessons. You might notice that we have changed the accessor of the color variable to **protected**. Protected allows subclasses to access this variable.

```
public class Car {
    protected String color = "";

    public Car(String tempColor) {
        color = tempColor;
    }

    public void displayInformation() {
        System.out.println("Car: The color of this car is "
                + color);
    }
}
```

This is our super class. Now we will get more specific by adding a couple of subclasses that inherit from *Car*.

```
public class Lamborghini extends Car {
    private int numberOfCylinders=0;

    public void Lamborghini(int tempNumberOfCylinders, String
tempColor) {
        super(tempColor);
        numberOfCylinders = tempNumberOfCylinders;
    }

    public void displayInformation() {
        System.out.println("Lamborghini:  The color of this car is "
+ color + " and the number of cylinders is "
            + numberOfCylinders);
    }
}
```

```
public class Ferrari extends Car {
    private int numberOfCylinders= 0;

    public Ferrari(int tempNumberOfCylinders, String tempColor) {
        super(tempColor);
        numberOfCylinders = tempNumberOfCylinders;
    }

    public void displayInformation() {
        System.out.println("Ferrari: The color of this car is "
                + color + " and the number of cylinders is "
                + numberOfCylinders);
    }
}
```

Notice that both *Lamborghini* and *Ferrari* have *Car* in parenthesis. That means that they inherit from *Car*. All three of these classes have a constructor. The first line in the subclasses constructors call the **super** class's constructor and pass it a value for *color*. The rest of the classes are pretty straight forward.

Now let's look at how they can be used in a program. Within our program we are going to declare and create an object instance of the *Lamborghini* class.

```
Lamborghini lamb = new Lamborghini(12, "Red");
lamb.displayInformation();
```

We are using this class in pretty much the same way we used *Car* in previous lessons. One thing that we should call out is that we set *lamb.color* but if you look at the *Lamborghini* class, it doesn't have a *color* variable. That is because *Lamborghini* and *Ferrari* inherit that variable from their parent, *Car*.

The power of inheritance is that we don't have to reinvent the wheel for each class we create. When there really is an "Is a" relationship, we are able to use inheritance to reuse functionality that exists in another class.

Learn Polymorphism

Learn about polymorphism, one of the tenets of object-oriented coding.

While the name, "Polymorphism", sounds really complicated, it isn't actually that tough. It has to do with the computer determining the type of an object at the time the program is running. Key to polymorphism is the way your program is set up. It will use inheritance in a specific way.

You've already learned about using inheritance in the last section. We will use the same *Car* types when we learn about polymorphism. In the last section we set up a super class called *Car* and two sub classes called *Lamborghini* and *Ferrari*.

For our example we will declare an array of *Cars* and add a bunch of different types of cars to the array.

```
public static void main(String[] args) {
  Car myCarArray[] = {new Lamborghini(12, "Red"),
      new Ferrari(10, "Green"),
      new Lamborghini(12, "Pink"),
      new Ferrari(10, "Blue"),
      new Car("Yellow")};
}
```

With five elements in our array, we can show the power of polymorphism. We are going to use a **for each** loop to step through the elements within the array. For each element in the array, we will call it's *displayInformation()* method.

The power of polymorphism is that the computer will figure out the type of the object and determine which *displayInformation()* method to call on its own. If we add the below lines within the main() method we can see the results.

```
for (Car car : myCarArray) {
    car.displayInformation();
}
```

When the program is executed, the output will look like this.

```
Lamborghini:  The color of this car is Red and the number of
cylinders is 12
Ferrari: The color of this car is Green and the number of cylinders
is 10
```

```
Lamborghini:  The color of this car is Pink and the number of
cylinders is 12
Ferrari: The color of this car is Blue and the number of cylinders is
10
Car: The color of this car is Yellow
```

See how different *displayInformation()* methods are displayed based on the type of the object?

The keys to setting polymorphism up are to have several classes that inherit from a super class. Notice when we declared the array it was the type of the super class (*Car*). This is really important. Also notice that in the **for** loop we treat all of the elements of the array as if they were the super class. We also have to make sure we have common methods across super and subclasses. *displayInformation()* is implemented in all three classes. When these things are found together you have polymorphism.

My Media Collection

This exercise helps you learn objects, inheritance, and polymorphism using a media collection.

If you know me, you know that I love my media. I have a ton of different types of media including cassettes, records, and CDs.

You are tasked with creating a collection of media with these types. You will want to use an array to store the media. The three types above will inherit from a super class called Media. Media will have a base set of variables and methods and each of the other types will have other unique variables and methods. All of the types, including Media, will have a display method.

Put together a program that implements the media collection as described above. Try to use polymorphism in your program.

Go into the Java IDE and create this program.

Russian Roulette Using Objects

This exercise helps you learn branching, looping, and objects as they implement Russian Roulette.

Russian Roulette is where a person takes a revolver with a single bullet in it. They spin the cylinder, aim the gun at a target, and pull the trigger.

Create a program that creates the Russian Roulette practice using the below details.

1. The location of the bullet in the six chamber revolver is selected at random.
2. The cylinder is spun and the selected chamber is decided at random.
3. The gun is aimed at the target and the trigger is pulled
4. The result is displayed to the user.
5. The user is asked if they want to try again.
6. If so, the trigger is pulled again.
7. Use an object-oriented approach to implementing this program.

Go into the Java IDE and create this program.

Learn Files

Learn how to use files to write and read data in your programs.

Loading and saving data from a file within your program can enhance the robustness of the user experience. All of our programs prior to this lesson have required that the user enter data each time the program runs. While this is fine for a guessing game or a calculator, , if I must reenter all of my cassettes, records, and CDs into my media collection each time the program runs, I am going to be pretty grumpy.

Incorporating files into our programs allow us to store data from a program to a file that can then be loaded again from the file the next time our program runs.

Any time we want to use a file, we first need to open the file. If our program was going to open a file for output (saving data to a file) our code would look like this.

```
try {
    FileWriter writer = new FileWriter("mytestfile.txt");
} catch (IOException ex) {
    System.err.println(ex.getMessage());
}
```

By the way, you will want to add `import java.io.*;` at the top of your program to use some of the classes we've included.

We will talk about the **try/catch** pieces in a minute here. To begin with, we will discuss the **FileWriter** line. **FileWriter** is a class in Java built to write to files. You create an object instance of it like we talked about in our Objects section. The constructor includes the path and name of your file. For this example I chose a simple file name without a path, but you might need to include the path. If you use the '\' symbol in your path, you will want to use two of them '\\' together. '\' is a special character in Java used for pattern matching. Putting two together tells Java to treat it like a normal symbol.

Now on to **try/catch**. The **try** block and the **catch** block help us when something doesn't go quite right when our program is running. Let's say you were trying to write a file to a place that didn't exist or you didn't have access to. **Try** tells Java to watch for possible problems. **Catch** tells Java how to filter problems that do happen and then what to do with them. Our **catch** block tells Java to look for the **IOException** problem. If one of these problems occur, our program will write to the error console (kind of like the output 'out' console we are used to) so we know what the problem is.

For an output stream we will want to **write** data to the file. We do it like this.

```
writer.write("My First Record");
```

The above statement is similar to a **println** statement but writes to a file instead. You can write a literal string like in the example above or you can include a variable name.

For all file-related operations, you need to make sure you **close** the file when you are done. Leaving a file open wastes system resources and can result in a memory leak. Here is how you close the file.

```
writer.close();
```

We have talked about an output stream. Now let's discuss using an input stream. An input stream **reads** data from a file that already exists. If the file doesn't exist, your program will probably throw an error. You will find that the syntax to open an input stream is very close to the output stream.

```
try {
    FileReader reader = new FileReader("mytestfile.txt");
} catch (IOException ex) {
    System.err.println(ex.getMessage());
}
```

The code to read from our file is a little different than to write because it reads a character at a time. Here is what it looks like to read the file.

```
int myChar;
while ((myChar = reader.read()) != -1) {
    System.out.print((char)myChar);
}
```

The **read** method in our program is within the **while** loop. As we read from the file, we check to see if it gets a -1. When it gets a -1, that tells us that we have reached the end of the file. Since it is reading a character at a time, we use a **print** method rather than **println** to print the data out.

To close the open file this time we use this code.

```
reader.close();
```

If you were to run the output stream code and then the input stream code and display the value of *myChar*, it would look like this.

```
My First Record
```

Here is the entire program using an Object based approach to read and write to a file.

```java
import java.io.*;
public class FileTest {
  String fileName;
  public FileTest(String tempFile) {
    fileName = tempFile;
  }
  public void writeFile() {
    try {
      FileWriter writer = new FileWriter(fileName);
      writer.write("My First Record");
      writer.close();
    } catch (IOException ex) {
      System.err.println(ex.getMessage());
    }
  }
  public void readFile() {
    try {
      FileReader reader = new FileReader(fileName);
        int myChar;
        while ((myChar = reader.read()) != -1) {
          System.out.print((char)myChar);
        }
        reader.close();
    } catch (IOException ex) {
        System.err.println(ex.getMessage());
    }
  }

  public static void main(String[] args) {
    FileTest fileTest = new FileTest("testfile.txt");
    fileTest.writeFile();
    fileTest.readFile();
  }
}
```

While there are other operations like deleting and renaming files, we have been able to work through the most common operations a programmer will typically perform. Adding file operations to your program can add significant benefit to your users.

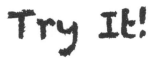

My Improved Media Collection

This exercise will help you to use files to improve your media collection program.

I've been using the great media collection program you put together earlier but am kind of getting tired of retyping all of my media into the program each time it runs.

For this exercise, enhance the media collection program written earlier to write the collection to a file at the end of the program and read the collection from the file at the beginning.

One thing you are going to need to consider is how you store the type of the media in the file and how you repopulate the array using the correct object types.

Go into the Java IDE and create this program.

REFERENCE

Java Reference

This workbook will use the following Java syntax.

Variable Declarations	```int``` variableName = 10;
	```String``` arrayName[] = {"bob","ann","fred","lisa");
	or
	```String``` arrayName = ```new String```[10];
	
	Types: ```int, float, string, boolean```

Variable Assignments	variableName = Assignment; arrayName[index] = Assignment;

Arithmetic Expression	+ Addition
	- Subtraction
	* Multiplication
	/ Division
	% Modulus
	^ Exponent
	```Math.Pow``` Exponent
	```java.util.Random.randint```(1,10) calculates random number between 1 and 10

Output	```System.out.println```(Item); ```System.out.println```(Item + Item);

Input	```import java.util.*;```
	```Scanner``` input = ```new Scanner(System.in);```
	
	variableName = input.```nextLine```();
	variableName = input.```nextInt```();

Logical Expressions	> Greater than
	< Less than
	>= Greater than or equal
	<= Less than or equal
	== Equal
	!= Not equal
	```AND```
	```OR```
	```NOT```

Branching	```if``` (logical expression)

```
                    Statements

          if (logical expression)
              Statements
          else
              Statements
```

Looping
```
          while (logical expression)
              Statements

          for (int variable = 0; variable < 10; variable++)
              Statements

          for (Object variable : arrayName)
              Statements
```

Methods
```
          public void methodName([Type][ParameterName], ...)
              Statements
              [return Value]

          methodName(Value)
          variableName = methodName(Value)
```

Classes
```
          public class ClassName [extends SuperClass]
              Variable and method definitions

          ClassName className = new ClassName();

          className.variable;
          className.method();
```

Files
```
          import java.io.*;

          FileWriter writer = new FileWriter(fileName);
          FileReader reader = new FileReader(fileName);

          writer.write("message");

          int myChar;
          while ((myChar = reader.read()) != -1)
              System.out.print((char) myChar);

          try {
              Statements
          } catch (IOException ex) {
              System.err.println(ex.getMessage());
          }
```

Other Coding Language References

Below is a list of references to common coding languages. You might want to use these references to help you do the exercises in this workbook using another language.

Language	Link to Reference
Java	https://docs.oracle.com/javase/10/docs/api/overview-summary.html
Python	https://docs.python.org/2.7/reference/index.html
Visual Basic	https://docs.microsoft.com/en-us/dotnet/visual-basic/language-reference/
C	https://www.gnu.org/software/gnu-c-manual/gnu-c-manual.html
Scratch	https://download.scratch.mit.edu/ScratchReferenceGuide14.pdf

Printed in Great Britain
by Amazon

84996979R00038